# ROBOTS

**CLIVE GIFFORD**

with illustrations by

**FRANK PICINI**

**CARLTON**

# WHAT'S A BOT?

**A** robot is a particularly amazing type of machine. Robots, or "bots" for short, are designed to carry out tasks without human help. In their brief history, robots have travelled to places no human can reach, taken on extraordinary jobs and changed the lives of many people. Yet most robot experts agree that the story of robots is only just beginning.

*Cog is a human-like robot with cameras for eyes. It uses information from these cameras to judge distances.*

## AMAZING ABILITIES

Most robots don't look like humans, but many can perform human-like actions with greater strength or efficiency than we can. Some bots are able to lift loads as heavy as 1,000 kg (just over 1 ton), while others can perform surgical operations with more accuracy than a human hand. Robots can be instructed or programmed to perform a variety of tasks. They can react to events around them and often operate entirely on their own.

*Cye is a small robot with many abilities. It vacuums carpets, carries items around the house and keeps a watchful eye on the home with its video cameras.*

## LOOK, LISTEN AND LEARN

Robots find out about their surroundings by using sensors. These are devices such as video cameras and proximity sensors, which judge how far away an object is. All this information is not much use unless the robot can use it to make decisions. The robot's controller, which is usually a computer, analyses the information, makes decisions and then sends instructions to the different parts of the robot so that it can react to its surroundings.

## LONG-DISTANCE OPERATORS

Some robots are tele-operated. This means that they are controlled from a distance by a human operator, but they still perform some parts of their tasks by themselves. The operator sends instructions to the robot from a remote-control unit or a tether-cable like that used by the underwater robot Jason Jr., or by beaming radio signals through space. Jason Jr. has explored and sent back videos and images of many shipwrecks, including that of the passenger liner RMS *Titanic*, which sank in 1912.

*Jason Jr. has been sent on top-secret missions to investigate the wrecks of sunken US Navy submarines. It uses grippers to pick up objects it finds inside the wrecks in order to transport them to the ocean surface.*

## ALL BY THEMSELVES

Most robots can perform a range of tasks without humans supervising their every move. Robots that are programmed to work entirely by themselves are said to be "autonomous". These robots have some intelligence, but researchers want to give them more. They want to create robots that can truly learn and think for themselves. This is called "artificial intelligence", or AI.

*This autonomous robot cleans floors at Manchester Airport in the UK. It moves through the airport terminals, busily going about its work without human help.*

## ON THE MOVE

All robots have the ability to move. Even factory robots that are bolted to the floor can twist and turn their arms or other parts. Some robots are fully mobile and able to dive underwater, fly through the air or move over the ground. Mobile robots on land often have wheels, but for uneven or rocky terrain they might have insect-like legs or caterpillar tracks like those on tanks. One robot, Robostrider, can even "walk on water" just like pond-skater insects. Another bot, RoboPike, can swim through water like a fish.

*RoboPike is 81 cm (32 in) long and has waterproof electric motors. The motors pull wires along the bot's body, making it swing from side to side in the water like a fish.*

## DID YOU KNOW?
Robostrider, the bot that walks on water, is built from a fizzy drinks can, stainless-steel wire legs and an elastic band fitted to a pulley to power its legs.

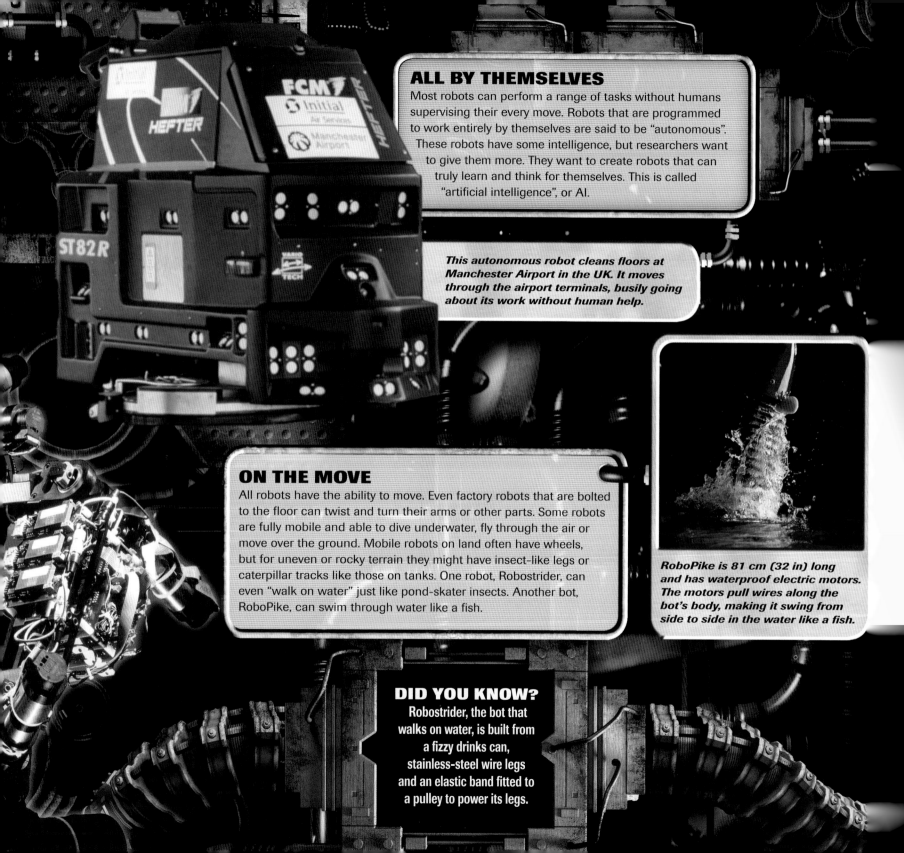

# BYGONE BOTS

The idea that machines can do the work of people is not new. For thousands of years, humans have been inventing labour-saving devices, such as the plough or potter's wheel. This drive to produce helpful machines, along with an age-old desire to create artificial beings similar to ourselves, resulted in the rise of robots. It was not until the arrival of electrical technology in the twentieth century that robots as we know them today really began to take off.

## AGE OF AUTOMATA

Long before the existence of robots, there were small, moving mechanical figures known as "automata". These developed from intricate spring, lever, gear and pulley-powered mechanisms used to make clocks. In about 1495, the Italian painter, sculptor and engineer Leonardo da Vinci sketched out – and may even have made – a mechanical knight full of cables and pulleys. This machine was designed to move in a human-like way, waving its arms, turning its head and opening and closing its visor.

*A model of da Vinci's armoured knight automaton (left) and its inner workings, produced from da Vinci's sketches.*

## MECHANICAL CREATURES

In the eighteenth century, engineers such as Frenchman Jacques de Vaucanson created automata with complicated moving parts – some could even draw or play a musical instrument! These contraptions astounded people at the time, but they were not real robots as they could not respond to the world around them.

*Vaucanson's "mechanical duck" had 400 moving parts and could flap its wings.*

## TWENTIETH-CENTURY ROBOTS

In the twentieth century, robots first appeared as imaginary beings in films, books and sci-fi magazines before they were actually built. From the 1920s, robot-like machines in human form began to be built for demonstrations. Although they seemed to react to the world around them, they were actually controlled by a person, or were upgrades of earlier automata but with flashing lights and other electrical gadgetry.

M·G·M PRESENTS
### FORBIDDEN PLANET
AMAZING!

*A poster featuring Robby the Robot, a character made famous in the popular 1950s' Forbidden Planet film.*

## DID YOU KNOW?

Jacques de Vaucanson was a priest before he became an engineer. He was thrown out of his religious order for making mechanical flying angels!

## MONSTER MACHINES

Robots as we know them appeared shortly after the invention of computers in the 1940s. Then computers were huge machines that filled entire rooms! Computers like ENIAC, EDVAC, Colossus and Konrad Zuse's Z3 were mostly used by the military and relied on thousands of electrical switch devices called relays that were bulky and unreliable. In the 1950s, when more advanced electrical parts such as transistors and silicon chips were introduced, computers became much smaller and far more powerful.

*The ENIAC computer took up an area of 63 sq m (680 sq ft). Its entire memory amounted to about 87.5 bytes. Today, a musical greetings card has more memory!*

## WESTINGHOUSE ELEKTRO

Elektro was a 2.14-m (7-ft) tall robot built in 1937 by Westinghouse, an American electrical company. It caused a sensation at public demonstrations, especially at the 1939 World's Fair held in New York. Beneath its aluminium skin were gears and a motor that made its head move, a 78-rpm record player so that it could appear to speak, and a set of air bellows that made the robot puff smoke when a cigarette was put in its mouth. Elektro's fame was short-lived. It disappeared from pubic view, only to be reassembled in 2004. Elektro is now on display in a museum in the United States.

*Elektro was accompanied by a mechanical dog, Sparko, that could walk, bark and turn its head on command.*

## DID YOU KNOW?

The very first hard disk drive appeared in 1957. It was built by IBM and was called the RAMAC Disk File. It featured fifty 60-cm (23-in) wide disks and weighed around 1000 kg (a ton). It held just 5 megabytes – $\frac{1}{140}$ th of the space found on a blank CD today.

*Unimate, the first industrial robot, took on jobs that were dangerous for factory workers.*

## REAL ROBOTS

In the 1950s and 1960s, as computers and electronics developed rapidly, the possibility of building proper robots became a reality. In 1956, two Americans, George Devol and Joseph Engelberger, formed the first robotics company, Unimation. Five years later, their Unimate robot was hard at work, lifting and moving red-hot steel castings in a General Motors car factory. It was the first fully programmable working robot, soon to be followed by thousands more in industry, space and underwater technology, and the military. By the 1990s, they were also in homes, schools and hospitals.

# OFF TO WORK

Some robots are designed for fun or for research in labs, but for millions of bots every day is a workday. Robots don't complain, need coffee breaks or take holidays. All they require is the occasional overhaul. There are two main types of working robot – industrial and service. Industrial robots work in factories, while service robots work in homes, offices and gardens.

## DULL, DIRTY AND DANGEROUS

The word "robot" comes from the Czech *robota*, meaning "drudgery". In factories, robots are replacing human workers who previously had to work in dull, dirty and sometimes dangerous jobs. Robots are capable of operating in fierce heat – close to a blast furnace in a steel factory – or in unpleasant conditions, such as in sewers. Once programmed, a robot can repeat its tasks over and over again with incredible accuracy. This makes them perfect for repetitive, dull jobs.

## INDUSTRIAL ROBOTS

Thousands of industrial robots have found work in car factories. There, they spray vehicle bodies with paint, weld (or fuse) parts together using heat, and help assemble complete vehicles. Driverless mobile robots known as "automated guided vehicles" (AGVs) trundle round the factory floor ferrying materials from one part of the factory to another. How do they know their way around the building? Some AGVs are programmed to follow a bright painted line on the ground using light sensors. Others can detect an electric signal from a guiding wire buried underneath the factory floor.

## JET SCRUBBER

The Skywash is a gigantic 33-m (108-ft) -long robot arm used by Germany's main airline, Lufthansa, to clean airliners. Two Skywashes take three hours to scrub a Boeing 747-400 jumbo jet – about a third of the time it takes human cleaners to perform the same task. It's the world's largest service robot.

## SPOT WELDING

Robot spot welders send a massive electric current (about 100 car-batteries' worth) through small spots on metal pieces so that the spots melt and join together. Robots are ideal for this job as it requires great accuracy. On a Mercedes-Benz A-Class car, around 3,900 spot welds have to be made to 290 different pieces of metal.

*A robot arm hard at work welding together vehicles in a Hyundai car factory in Beijing, China.*

## SERVICE ROBOTS

Many service robots perform jobs to help people in hospitals, offices, homes and gardens. Tasks such as cleaning swimming pools, floors and carpets, and mowing lawns can now be done by small mobile robots. These bots have sensors that can detect any obstacles in their way, from a chair to a pet dog!

*The Roomba robot floor-cleaner can navigate around a room collecting dirt without human help. In the future, robot cleaners may find keys and lost objects, act as a home security robot and even babysit children.*

In the future, more and more service robots will work closely with people. The first museum guides and receptionists are already coming into service, from the Wakamaru robot secretary in Japan to Sweetlips, a robot that guides people around the Carnegie Museum of Natural History in the United States. Someday, robots may act as store assistants in shops and even as teaching assistants in schools, where they could keep an eye on students and offer advice during lessons. Other bots are being developed to prepare and serve food and drink. A basic robot waiter has already begun working at the Robot Kitchen restaurant in Hong Kong.

*Mitsubishi's Wakamaru is a 1-m (3-ft) -high robot secretary on wheels. It can record notes, recognize 10 human faces and remind these people of their appointments.*

## CYNTHIA

Cynthia is a 2-m (6½-ft) -high robot bartender, built by robot designer Dick Becker. For four years it worked in Cynthia's Bar in London, where it served customers with drinks ordered from a control panel. Cynthia's two robot arms could pick up drinks bottles and mix 75 different cocktail drinks.

## IN THE GARDEN

Slugs beware: SlugBot is out to get you! This garden robot, built by scientists for research, seeks out slugs munching on garden plants. It picks them up with a three-fingered claw and drops them into a special tank in its trailer, where they quickly rot. The energy released by the rotting slugs is then converted into electricity to power SlugBot. Ingenious!

## DID YOU KNOW?

The Kuka Titan is the world's strongest industrial robot. Its arm, which can reach out 3.2 m (10 ½ ft), is able to lift a whopping 1,000 kg (2,200 lb).

## ROBOT ARMS

Each direction in which a robot arm moves is called a "degree of freedom", or DOF. Robots with several joints have more degrees of freedom. Many robot arms have a wrist joint that can go up and down, from side to side and roll round, adding three extra degrees of freedom.

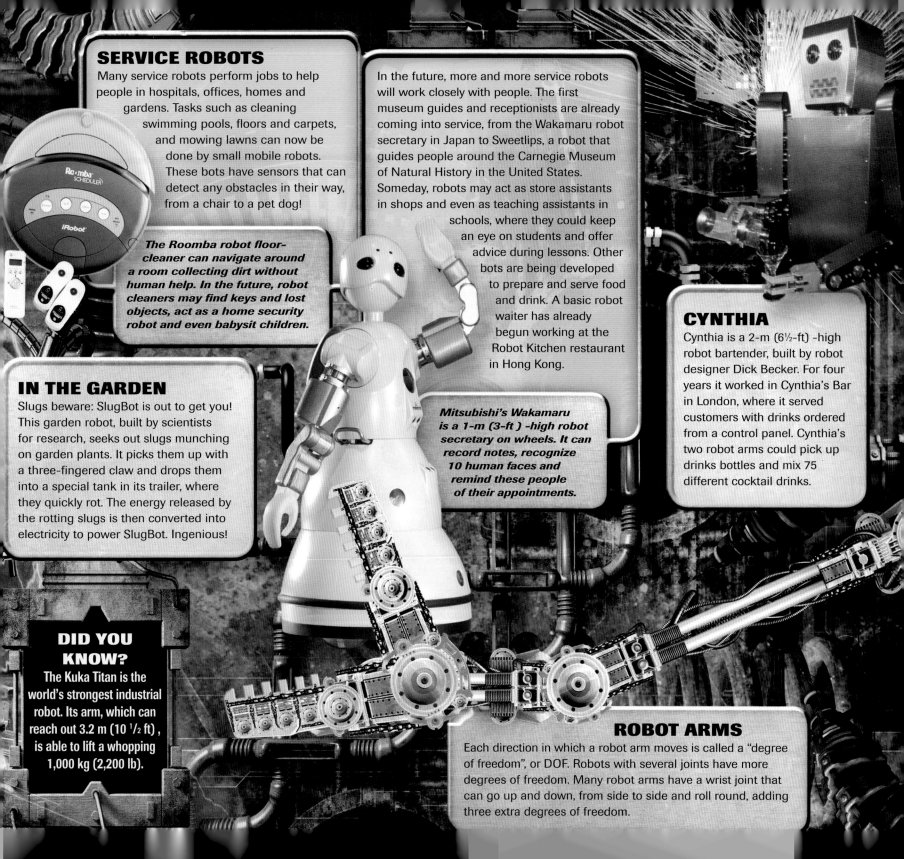

# DANGER!

**B**ad news for robots: unlike people, they are thoroughly replaceable! More and more robots are being put to work in places too risky for humans to set foot in. Handling bombs, travelling deep underwater, entering blazing buildings – here are the robots that risk everything each time they go on a mission.

## HAZARD ALERT!

Many robots are put into operation to help rescue people from disaster scenes, or to prevent catastrophe by defusing bombs or seeking out leaking poisonous gases. HazMat robots, for instance, work with hazardous material such as toxic chemicals. Some of them are sent down pipes looking for leaks; others, with feet that grip walls, clamber down into giant tanks full of chemicals. Other bots deal with nuclear waste that is highly radioactive, which means it can give out an energy that can kill living things! One industrial robot, Redzone Robotics' Rosie, helped dismantle a nuclear power reactor. Robots also check drums of radioactive waste for leakage. As old nuclear power stations are closed and dismantled in the future, this type of hazard robot is likely to become increasingly important.

*This snake-like robot can crawl down pipes, carrying cameras and sensors to look for cracks or gas leaks. Future snakebots may be used at disaster sites to weave their way through air ducts into a collapsed building.*

## FIRE! FIRE!

Heat, poisonous smoke and the threat of a building crashing down make fire-fighting a dangerous job. Robots are being developed to help firefighters tackle big blazes. Firerob has water cannons to fight fires in factories and tunnels. Fitted with a heat shield, it can withstand temperatures up to 1,250°C (2,282°F). The Japanese Guardrobo D1 is designed as a security robot to patrol buildings, looking for intruders, and to put out fires.

*Guardrobo D1 demonstrates its powerful fire-extinguishing cannon system.*

## TO THE RESCUE!

Rescue robots are often small and are able to crawl into gaps in rubble or damaged buildings at a disaster scene. They work their way through twisted steel and broken glass, carrying video cameras and sensors to warn those above of leaking gases that could catch fire or explode at any moment. They also have microphones and heat sensors to detect trapped survivors. Future rescue robots will even be equipped to pick up the signs of a person's pulse and breathing. They will also carry oxygen, water and medicines to keep survivors alive until they are fully rescued.

*This powerful tmsuk T52 Enryu rescue robot has two incredibly strong arms, each capable of tearing off a locked car door or lifting a weight of almost 500 kg (half a ton).*

## UNDER PRESSURE

Pressure increases sharply the deeper someone goes under water. Few unprotected human divers can travel more than 100 m (330 ft) deep, and at 2,000 m (6,560 ft) or more, an unprotected submarine can be crushed as if it were a tin can. Some underwater robots are built from incredibly strong materials, such as the metal titanium, so they can dive deep. There they check out ship- and plane-wrecks, recover salvage and search for new marine life. In 2004, a pair of French underwater robots, Scorpio and Super Achilles, dived in the Red Sea and recovered important flight-recorder instruments, known as "black boxes", from a crashed Boeing 737 airliner.

*The remotely operated Super Achilles retrieving ancient Roman pots from the Mediterranean sea.*

## TOP SECRET

In May 2007, Odyssey Marine Exploration announced that its robot, Zeus, had helped recover more than half a million silver coins from an ancient shipwreck in the Atlantic Ocean. The ship name and location remain top secret.

# BOMB!

*Equipped with a range of cameras, a bomb-disposal robot sends back close-up images to its human operators a safe distance away. Its grippers may be fitted with a key to open a door, a sharp metal spike to smash a window, or even a type of shotgun to blast away a door lock. Its arm may carry a range of end-effector tools. If the suspicious package is a briefcase, a two-fingered gripper is used to grab the object, but if the item is an irregular-shaped object, such as a bag or belt of explosives, a three-pronged device called a cat claw might be deployed. To destroy the bomb, some robots use a device called a "disrupter". This fires a narrow, but extremely powerful, jet of water into the bomb, disrupting its electrical circuits and stopping the bomb from blowing up.*

*A radio-controlled robot moves in and grabs a suspicious package with its gripper.*

# D.I.Y. DROIDS

## DO.IT.YOURSELF

**M**any people become so fascinated with robots that they decide to build their own. As well as a few tools and a range of parts, they need lots of ingenuity and imagination to come up with an idea for a robot – and the patience to get it to work.

## BUILDING A WORKING ROBOT

Building a bot involves constructing a robot body and giving it moving parts, which are usually powered by a number of small electric motors. The biggest challenge is working out how to link sensors and a controller so that the robot can react to events or its surroundings. Many simple robots use a device called a "BASIC Stamp microcontroller". This is a microchip, or a series of tiny electrical circuits, that can be linked to a personal computer. Simple programs to operate the robot can then be downloaded to the robot. Sensors used for home-built bots often include touch, or contact, sensors. These ensure that when a robot bumps into something, its motors make the robot turn or reverse. Other sensors include line-following sensors that let a robot travel along a marked-out path.

*One of the most difficult but exciting aspects of robot-making is working out how to link the small electronic parts to make the robot move.*

## ROBOT KITS

Making a robot from scratch is a major task. It requires lots of electronics knowledge to purchase the correct parts, design the circuits and join the components. For this reason, many complete beginners start with a robot kit. This makes things much easier and contains all the parts necessary to build one or more robots. One of the most successful types of robot kit is the LEGO MINDSTORMS® series. These kits are based around an RCX or NXT controller, which is fitted inside a large brick containing inputs and outputs for sensors. This can be loaded with programs via a transmitter. By using MINDSTORMS® and LEGO® bricks, robot-makers can design their own robots with their own special features.

*The NXT controller with its ultrasonic, light, sound and touch sensors (clockwise from bottom right). The three servomotors at the top allow the robot to move.*

### DID YOU KNOW?

Amateur robot-makers have created robots from all sorts of things, including old paint rollers, computer mice and floppy disk drives!

*Meet Spike, the MINDSTORMS® scorpion robot. When it hits a target with its stinger, it makes a noise.*

## BATTLE OF THE BOTS

Since the mid-1990s, robot enthusiasts have designed and built bots only to see them destroyed in combat-robot competitions! Events such as *Robot Wars* and *BattleBots* pit armoured robots against one another. Programmed to defend and attack, these bots are armed with weapons as varied as electric saws, large metal hammers and fork-lift arms that can get underneath a rival robot and flip it over.

*Flame-throwing bots battle it out in the popular TV programme Robot Wars.*

## DID YOU KNOW?

RoboGames, formerly the ROBOlympics, is the biggest robot competition in the world. The 2007 event in San Francisco, CA, USA, attracted hundreds of robots in 70 different events, from robot sumo wrestling to humanoid robot weightlifting.

## IN COMPETITION

Some robot-makers have entered their bots in competitions designed to test certain robot skills, such as the ability to navigate courses and avoid obstacles without human help. International micromouse competitions are some of the oldest examples, in which small robots cruise around a maze trying to find the centre in the shortest possible time. Robot soccer is also a terrific test for mobile robots. With this game they have to react as a team, follow the path of the ball, plot how to intercept it and score a goal. RoboCup is the World Cup of robot soccer.

*RoboCup has events for wheeled and humanoid robots of different sizes and complexity. In this version of RoboCup, teams of four robots play soccer on a 3 m x 5 m (10 ft x 16 ft) field. The robots use wireless networking to communicate.*

# SPY BOTS

In tests during the 1990s, Robart III was able to cruise through empty offices and warehouses, opening electronic doors and looking for intruders. Its gun could fire six tranquilizer darts in 1.5 seconds.

**W**atch out! There are cops and spies about, but they're not human! Police have long used machines and dogs to help in their investigations. Now they are turning to robots in their quest to patrol, tackle crime, spy on suspects and gain vital intelligence on terrorists and enemy forces.

The stair-climbing *ASENDRO SCOUT* robot assesses hazards in split-seconds. It homes in on suspicious people and suspect packages.

## ON ALERT

Compared to human security guards and spies, robotic sentries don't fall asleep, can operate 24 hours a day, aren't easily distracted and can sound the alarm instantly even while being attacked. Robots are currently used to patrol military facilities, high-tech laboratories and homes.

## HIGH-RISK HELPERS

Some security robots are sent to investigate dangerous areas, such as the hideout of a criminal gang. Others might be used to take a phone to hostage-takers so that police can contact them to try to free the hostages. In combat zones, robots like PackBots and Talon rovers have been sent in ahead of human soldiers. These robotic rovers check for lethal surprises, from booby traps and mines to enemy soldiers lurking around corners.

## SAFE AT HOME

Guard robots are also helping with security at home. Fujitsu's MARON-1 can follow a pre-programmed patrol path around a home. It can operate remote-controlled devices, such as TVs and garage doors, and sound an alarm if it detects smoke or unexpected movement. A four-legged robot, Banryu, performs similar tasks and is equipped with temperature, movement and sound sensors to detect fires or intruders.

*Banryu is a home-security robot that is operated from a cellphone. The word "Banryu" means "guard dragon".*

*MARON-1's swivelling eyeballs contain two cameras that take images of the inside of a house, or of an intruder, and send them to the owner's mobile phone.*

SICK

## THE FLYING, SPYING DOUGHNUT

*When people first spotted the Cypher, they thought it was a flying saucer! The Cypher was shaped like a doughnut, with helicopter rotor blades whirring around inside the hole in its 1.95-m (6-ft) wide body. It could hover outside the windows of a tall building and drop a radio or other surveillance equipment onto the roof. The Cypher made over 550 flights. Its successor, the Cypher II, can be fitted with wings for longer-distance missions.*

*The Cypher II could spy in through a skyscraper window while hovering outside.*

## SPIES IN THE SKY

Unmanned aerial vehicles, or UAVs, are in the skies, used by police and security forces to spy on the ground below. Police blimps, or small airships, travel slowly and use zoom cameras. At night the blimps use thermal imagers to detect objects.

*A Predator UAV in operation.*

Military UAVs, such as Global Hawk and MQ-1 Predator, cruise for hours at a time, taking hundreds of images of enemy bases or troop movements. Sentry Owl is a smaller UAV, weighing 5 kg (11 lb). It an be carried in a soldier's backpack and assembled in minutes. Future flying spies will be even smaller than Sentry Owl. Micro aerial vehicles (MAVs) that sit easily in a person's hand will be able to fly around unnoticed, homing in on targets and relaying crucial information.

## DID YOU KNOW?

At least three Global Hawk UAV spy planes have been lost in combat zones in the Middle East. Plans are afoot to power a new Global Hawk with a small nuclear reactor. This would give it virtually unlimited flying time.

*In thermal imaging, heat shows up as colour. The hottest area of the car in this thermal image is red, the coolest part is blue.*

*Scientists have at last discovered how insects fly – a fact that is likely to help the development of flying robots. The tiny Dragonfly robot is being developed to follow suspected criminals and guide missiles to their targets. It will also search inside collapsed buildings to find survivors in disaster or war situations.*

# ROBOTS IN SPACE

**W**hen people go into space, they need vast amounts of kit, food, water, air and other supplies. They also need to come back. However, space robots just need a power source to be able to work in hostile surroundings on other planets – and the chances are that they are not coming back.

## SPACE BUILDERS

High above you, orbiting the Earth at an average speed of over 27,780 km/h (17,200 mph), is the biggest-ever building site in space. The International Space Station will be completed in 2010, when it will weigh over 213,000 kg (233 tons), be over 58 m (190 ft) long and fitted with 73-m (240-ft) -wide solar panels. This huge building project is being worked on by robots, including free-flying robot cameras and the 17.7-m (58-ft) -long SSRMS robot arm, used for moving equipment and supplies.

*A NASA astronaut anchored to the SSRMS robot arm during a space walk in 2005.*

## SPACE FLEETS

NASA (the National Aeronautics and Space Administration) is working on a team of robots that can be flown to Mars when it is at its closest, about 56 million km (35 million miles) away. One day, scores of robots capable of putting themselves together might be flown in giant space fleets to build a space-colony base in preparation for a first visit by humans!

*Future missions may make use of a humanoid robot, Robonaut (left), with its camera-filled head, and arms and hands capable of performing delicate tasks. Robonaut is packed with sensors (more than 150 per arm) that can detect temperature, touch, force and the robot's location.*

## A NEW HOME

Currently, a spacecraft takes many decades just to leave our solar system. Reaching another star system could take thousands of years. Future bots may have to be put in "sleeper" or "standby" mode for centuries as they are sent on massive missions to find new planets for future people to colonize. Perhaps the ultimate challenge for space robots would be to alter the entire environment of Mars or another planet to enable life to survive there.

Known as "terraforming", this might involve millions of robots making and pumping out gases to form a life-supporting atmosphere. Other robots may work drilling for minerals, searching for water underground, melting ice caps to produce liquid water, and tending plants and bacteria to create the right conditions for humans.

*An artist's impression of spider-like robots on Mars. Robots like these may one day "terraform" distant planets.*

AERCam Sprint is a free-flying robot ball designed to carry out tasks that are dangerous and time-consuming for astronauts. Sprint has two cameras that beam back images to astronauts safe inside a spacecraft.

Launched in 1972, Pioneer 10 was the first space probe to send back close-up pictures of Jupiter.

The spacecraft/probe Cassini-Huygens took seven years to reach Saturn in 2004, where it discovered five new moons.

# OUT OF THIS WORLD

Space probes are unmanned spacecraft, many of which have robotic features packed with technology and experiments, that are sent out to investigate the solar system.

The Rosetta space probe will reach the comet 67P/Churyumov-Gerasimenko in 2014, where it will drop a robot lander to ride piggyback on the comet.

## DID YOU KNOW?

Sojourner was the first roving robot on Mars but it moved painfully slowly – just a centimetre (third of an inch) every second, which equals 36 m (118 ft) per hour!

## MOVING ON MARS

Mars' lack of oxygen and water, and temperature swings of 100ºC (212ºF) per day, make it incredibly hostile for humans, so probes orbit the planet, and robot rovers like Sojourner (launched in 1997), and Spirit *(right)* and Opportunity (both launched in 2004), are sent to travel around its surface. Radio signals take several minutes to reach Mars from Earth, so a probe has to make instant decisions for itself. Spirit and Opportunity are packed with sensors and tools, including a small robot arm that can grind away outer rock so that other instruments can analyse the rock underneath.

# LIFESAVERS

**R**obot doctors and nurses may sound a bit scary but they're already on the wards, helping to save lives and bringing comfort to patients in hospitals.

## MEDICAL ROBOTS

One of the ways that robots are already saving lives is through microsurgery – operating on tiny parts of the body with ultra-small tools. It means that surgeons no longer have to cut patients' bodies wide open to operate and can tackle very delicate parts of the body, such as the eyes and brain, more easily. Outside the operating theatre, robots are also speeding up work in hospitals. Some robots offer around-the-clock care for the elderly and other patients who need lots of attention.

## MICROSURGERY

In robotic microsurgery, human surgeons control extremely accurate robot arms that have surgical tools, such as scalpels or clamps, attached to them. The precise, rock-steady movements of a robot can be controlled to within fractions of a millimetre and, unlike human surgeons, robot arms and hands don't shake or get tired.

## DA VINCI SYSTEM

One of the most successful robots has been the da Vinci Surgical System. It is made up of four robot arms that are fitted to a special patient cart. The arms are controlled by a surgeon sitting at a console. The surgeon sees a highly magnified, 3-D view of the operation on the console's screen, and controls the robots' movements with high-tech joysticks using "motion scaling". In motion scaling, the surgeon's hand movements of one or two centimetres in any direction are scaled down to a millimetre or fraction of a millimetre by the robot arms.

*In 2006, da Vinci Surgical Systems robots performed more than 48,000 operations.*

## LONG-DISTANCE DOCTOR

On 7 September 2001, an amazing operation was performed using the Zeus surgery robot. The robot removed the gall-bladder of a female patient in Strasbourg, France. Amazingly, the doctor overseeing the surgery, Jacques Marescaux, was on the other side of the Atlantic Ocean in New York. Fast radio signals ensured that the operation was a success.

*The robotic handles of the Zeus Surgical System are controlled in much the same way as joysticks are used to control the action of a video game.*

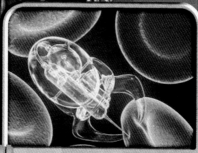

*An artist's impression of a nanobot that can inject a drug into an infected cell inside a human body.*

*One day, tiny nanobots may travel through the body to fight disease and infection.*

### DID YOU KNOW?

Robodoc is a robot that drills an incredibly accurate hole down a leg bone to fit an artificial hip implant. It has already performed over 1,500 operations.

## HOSPITAL HELPERS

Nurse-bots like Pearl, Flo and Care-O-bot II respond to patients' needs by reacting to voice commands or display options on a touchscreen. The bots bring food, drink and medicine, check a patient's condition and alert a doctor if there is a problem. Robots like HOSPI and Helpmate resemble the AGVs (automated guided vehicles) used in factories. Programmed with a map of the medical centre they work in, these robots ferry bed linen, equipment, bandages and other medical supplies around. Other robots, like Homerus and Robot RX, prepare hundreds of medical prescriptions each day. They receive orders from doctors and use a barcode scanner similar to that in a supermarket checkout to select the correct medicines.

*Nurse-bots such as Pearl enable health workers to interact with patients from a distance.*

## WORKING FROM THE INSIDE

In March 2007, researchers in Canada managed to send a tiny wireless robot down a blood artery at a speed of 10 cm (4 in) per second. This experiment could lead to a major breakthrough in what is known as robot "nanotechnology". "Nanorobots", measuring tiny fractions of millimetres, may be put into the body through the mouth or another small opening. These microscopic robots could replace scans as a way of investigating problems in the body. They could also test cells, blood and tissue for diseases and other problems. As they will work directly at the source of the problem, they will save time and lives. Nanotechnology may even result in hundreds of unbelievably small robots crammed into a pill that can fight blood clots, cancer and other diseases once inside the body.

# HALF-HUMAN,

In recent times, artificial, or "prosthetic", limbs have become more lifelike. Some, fitted with microchips, or tiny electrical circuits, have also become smarter. At the same time, more and more artificial body parts have been fitted inside people, ranging from hip-bone replacements to artificial hearts. As technology and robotics advance, will we eventually become part-machine, part-human?

## CYBORGS

The word "cyborg" is short for "cybernetic organism", meaning someone who is part-human, part-machine. The word "cyborg" means different things to different people. To scientists or doctors, it may explain the everyday matter of adding artificial body-parts to disabled people to help them regain normal human abilities. The results are known as "restorative cyborgs". To other people, the word "cyborg" conjures up sci-fi scenes of people upgraded with technology to gain almost super-human powers. These are called "enhanced cyborgs".

## SUPER-HUMAN POWERS

Human beings have skeletons on the inside of their bodies, known as "endoskeletons". Insects have "exoskeletons", which are supporting frameworks on the outside of their bodies. Robotic exoskeletons built for human use magnify the powers or strength of the human who "wears" them. In Japan, Tsukuba University is working on an exoskelton for disabled people known as HAL-5. In the USA, Berkeley University's BLEEX has piston-powered metal leg-braces that make walking with a heavy load easy.

As technology advances, it could be possible to produce enhanced cyborgs with amazing new abilities. Future eye surgery may not just remove the need to wear glasses, it might also bring about the power of night vision. Artificial limbs may come with robotic abilities, making them incredibly strong, fast-moving and precise.

*A student from Tsukuba University demonstrates the HAL-5 suit.*

*Shadow Hand, produced by Shadow Robot Company, is the most accurate replica of the human hand ever made.*

## DID YOU KNOW?

The first artificial body parts for humans are at least 3,400 years old. Archaeologists have discovered an ancient Egyptian mummy with an artificial toe on its foot!

# HALF-MACHINE

## MIND-CONTROL ARMS

In 2001, an American man called Jesse Sullivan received a huge electric shock from a power cable and, as a result, had to have both his arms amputated. He was fitted with a microchip-controlled robotic arm connected to his nerves. This means he can control the arm with his brain in a similar way to a real arm. In 2006, Claudia Mitchell was injured in a motorcycle accident and became the first woman to use a similar arm.

*Jesse Sullivan and Claudia Mitchell demonstrate their robot arms.*

## PROJECT CYBORG 2.0

In 1998, robotics expert Kevin Warwick stopped working on robots and started experimenting on himself. He had a small microprocessor chip implanted into his arm that could transmit signals that opened electronic doors. Project Cyborg 2.0, which began four years later, was more ambitious. This time the implant was connected to a nerve in Warwick's left arm. It could sense the tiny electrical signals along the nerve sent by his brain and transmit them to a computer. When the computer was hooked up to the Internet, Warwick could control a robot arm on the other side of the Atlantic Ocean by using his thoughts alone.

*The inner workings of Claudia Mitchell's high-tech, thought-controlled arm.*

*Kevin Warwick has written up his latest electronic-implant experiment in the book I, Cyborg.*

## BRAINS – AT A PRICE!

Memory-chip implants that link directly to the brain may enable a person to speak another language instantly or become hugely knowledgeable on a subject. But, like plastic surgery, this kind of technology may only be available to the wealthy.

# A.I. ARTIFICIAL INTELLIGENCE

**A**rtificial intelligence (AI) is all about making machines think and act in intelligent ways. It's a complex field of study involving all sorts of different sciences, not only electronics but also the sciences that look at how the human mind works.

## BRAIN POWER

Intelligence involves being able to work things out using your own experience and learning, even with only a little bit of information. Giving robots the ability to learn is one way to give robots artificial intelligence. Although this technology is still new, robots like COG, Robota and Lucy (the robot orang-utan) are already capable of learning simply through their vision, sound and touch sensors.

*Man vs machine: Deep Blue II's form of artificial intelligence was known as "brute force". It described the computer's ability to process 200 million chess positions per second. Kasparov is on the left.*

## EXPERIENCE AND LEARNING

In order to play a game of chess, a human being needs to have a level of intelligence and experience. Computers can play chess by running through thousands of different moves per second to decide what move to make next. The end result can be impressive. In 1997, IBM's Deep Blue II computer beat the chess world champion Garry Kasparov three games to two, with one game drawn in a six-game series.

People are not born with a complete understanding of the game of chess or the world around them already stored in their brains. Instead, they spend their lives learning and building up experience about the world (and chess). Many experts think that trying to build robots that start out "stupid" but can learn in similar ways to humans will lead to true artificial intelligence.

*Built by British robot enthusiast Steve Grand, Lucy is an orang-utan-like robot that is slowly trying to learn the meanings of words it hears and objects it sees with its one camera.*

## ROBO QUOTE:

*"Artificial intelligence is the science of making machines do things that require intelligence if done by men."*
AI pioneer
Marvin Minsky

## FUTURE AI

Is it possible to build a single robot that is aware that it exists and can think and act with intelligence in all the different ways that a human can? No one knows just yet, but if it were possible it would create a revolution in robotics and in society. Full AI robots would be in demand in all walks of life. They may even work as journalists in the world's hot spots or become the ultimate space explorers and law enforcers!

Some AI experts are following a different, exciting path. They aim to distribute intelligence among a large number of robots to form a robot "swarm". Each member of this large robot group could have a different type of intelligence or skill. By communicating with one another, the robots could share their skills and knowledge to form a powerful, super-intelligent team.

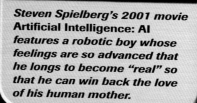

*Steven Spielberg's 2001 movie Artificial Intelligence: AI features a robotic boy whose feelings are so advanced that he longs to become "real" so that he can win back the love of his human mother.*

## SUPER DRIVERLESS CAR

*Stanley is no ordinary Volkswagen Touareg car. It is an intelligent robot vehicle that can navigate and drive itself without remote control or human help. In 2005, the Stanford Racing Team entered Stanley in one of the toughest AI tests, the DARPA (Defence Advance Research Projects Agency) Grand Challenge held in the USA. This race between different types of autonomous robot cars was held over 212 km (132 miles) of tough desert terrain. Stanley completed the course and scooped the two-million-dollar first prize!*

*Stanley navigated the 2005 Grand Challenge course successfully by using many sensors that fed data to computers fitted inside its boot. Its steering wheel was moved by an electric motor.*

**DID YOU KNOW?**
The 2007 DARPA Urban Challenge was set in a mock urban area where the robots had to understand and obey all traffic laws, including stopping at traffic lights.

The Actroid is a humanoid robot that looks and acts like a person. It may not have AI, but it can recognize certain words and phrases, blink its eyes and turn its head to make eye contact with whoever is speaking to it.

## LIVING DOLLS

ROBOTA dolls are mini-robots with simple AI. They have been developed as educational robots that can interact with humans by "seeing", speaking and imitating human speech, behaviour and gestures.

From ancient wooden puppets to modern computer characters in online games, people have long been fascinated with making versions of themselves. It is no surprise, then, that many research robots are humanoids, or human-like robots. The researchers' ultimate aim is to create a humanoid robot with artificial intelligence (AI). Yet, there are plenty of challenges apart from AI to overcome before a true humanoid companion can be produced.

*This Partner Ballroom Dance Robot cannot perform actual dance steps, as it has three wheels not feet. However, it is able to react to and copy the movements of its human partner's upper body.*

## COMPLEX CREATURES

Human beings are highly complicated creatures with flexible movement a complex brain fed information by the nervous system and powerful senses. Recreating the complete range of human abilities and senses in a robot is a massive challenge, but one that researchers are trying to tackle piece by piece.

## SPORTY BOTS

Just getting a robot to walk well on two legs and keep its balance is difficult. But today, many humanoids can now walk and climb stairs with relative ease. Sony's QRIO robot can dance, while several experimental robots, including HOAP-2 and Morph 3, are capable of performing martial arts moves from karate and kick-boxing. With artificial muscles on the way to making robot movement fast and flexible, the distant future may see robots act as playing partners or coaches for humans playing sports.

## DID YOU KNOW?

One Japanese robot, Robovie-II, has been fitted with a touch-sensitive skin made of layers of silicone rubber over a sensor. This skin allows the robot to judge where it was touched and with how much force. Poke Robovie II hard and it will say, "Ow!"

*Designed to mimic human muscles, TRON-X is driven by 200 pneumatic (air-powered) cylinders. By controlling the cylinders, a human operator can make the robot dance, change facial expressions and make hand gestures.*

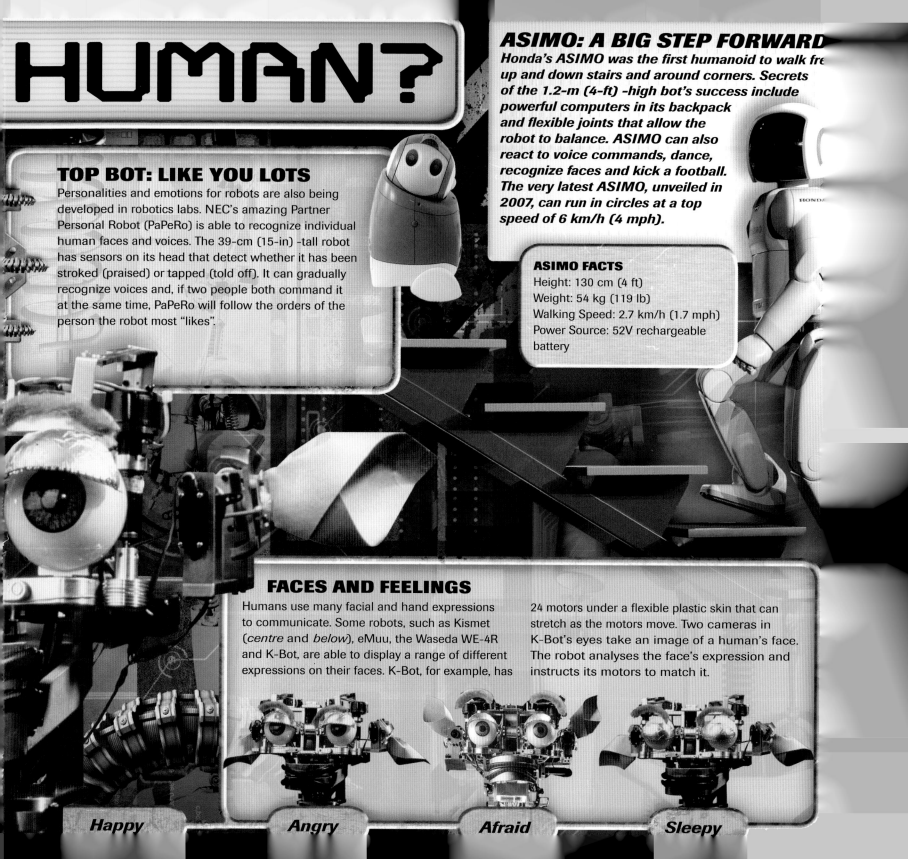

# HUMAN?

## ASIMO: A BIG STEP FORWARD

Honda's ASIMO was the first humanoid to walk freely up and down stairs and around corners. Secrets of the 1.2-m (4-ft) -high bot's success include powerful computers in its backpack and flexible joints that allow the robot to balance. ASIMO can also react to voice commands, dance, recognize faces and kick a football. The very latest ASIMO, unveiled in 2007, can run in circles at a top speed of 6 km/h (4 mph).

## TOP BOT: LIKE YOU LOTS

Personalities and emotions for robots are also being developed in robotics labs. NEC's amazing Partner Personal Robot (PaPeRo) is able to recognize individual human faces and voices. The 39-cm (15-in) -tall robot has sensors on its head that detect whether it has been stroked (praised) or tapped (told off). It can gradually recognize voices and, if two people both command it at the same time, PaPeRo will follow the orders of the person the robot most "likes".

### ASIMO FACTS
Height: 130 cm (4 ft)
Weight: 54 kg (119 lb)
Walking Speed: 2.7 km/h (1.7 mph)
Power Source: 52V rechargeable battery

## FACES AND FEELINGS

Humans use many facial and hand expressions to communicate. Some robots, such as Kismet (*centre* and *below*), eMuu, the Waseda WE-4R and K-Bot, are able to display a range of different expressions on their faces. K-Bot, for example, has 24 motors under a flexible plastic skin that can stretch as the motors move. Two cameras in K-Bot's eyes take an image of a human's face. The robot analyses the face's expression and instructs its motors to match it.

*Happy*          *Angry*          *Afraid*          *Sleepy*

# ROBOT DESTINY

**T**echnology is moving fast. Sixty years ago, there were no real-life robots. Forty years ago, no one had a personal computer. Two decades ago, there was no World Wide Web. In the future, scientists plan to create humanoids and other bots equipped with artificial intelligence. What else is likely to happen to robots, people and the world in the next century and beyond?

## A ROBOT POPULATION

For robots to have a major impact on Earth, they need to be produced in large numbers, in much the same way that other consumer goods, such as TVs and cars, are today. If that were to happen, people would find themselves living alongside a large robot population. Future robot-making factories may be artificially intelligent and capable of churning out thousands of machines without human help. The first batches of AI robots made in the factories would assemble themselves. Some of these intelligent bots may stay on as supervisors to build and run the factory, while others could transport themselves for sale.

## DID YOU KNOW?

In 2003, a nanotechnology researcher at Cornell University, USA, made a playable nano-guitar with strings the size of a red blood cell.

## CHILD OF THE FUTURE?

Picture this: In 2250 a baby's first breath may be taken in the arms of a robot with warm, flexible silicone rubber skin. A robot surgeon may implant identity chips in the baby's body. The child may not go to school, but be taught by home robot tutors instead. When the child is old enough, other bots could monitor how it plays with other children. These bots could assess the child's development and advise on what career he or she should follow.

*In the movie I, Robot, set on Earth in 2035, advanced humanoid robots with AI are mass-produced in factories like cars.*

## SMILEY FACE

*Glad to see a friendly face? This robotic face can smile on command and could be the basis for a museum guide, receptionist or care-bot of the future.*

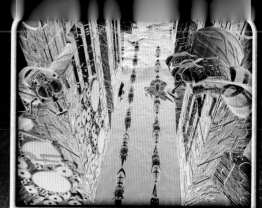

*An artist's impression of a nanorobot city of the future. Wasplike and antlike nanorobots zoom around the streets, all carrying out different tasks.*

## NANOTECHNOLOGY

Nanotechnology is the science of building to a very tiny scale. One nanometre is equal to one millionth of a millimetre. A single human hair has a diameter of 80,000 nanometres! In the distant future, tiny robots, or nanobots, may construct themselves in their millions inside nano-factories housed in a single room. Nanobots may have a great impact on human health, in the form of medical bots (see *Lifesavers*). But produced in vast numbers, nanobots may also be capable of battling against environmental problems – by removing pollution from water, or repairing the hole in the ozone layer in the Earth's atmosphere.

*Could swarms of nanorobots co-exist happily with humans?*

## ROBOT FRIENDS

Robots of the future might provide humans with entertainment as sports trainers or partners in leisure activities. Humans and their robot companions will also be able to access the world's knowledge via incredibly fast wireless links.

*SARCOS, a humanoid robot used at entertainment displays, can paint and even play cards. This robot is pre-programmed, but future robots may be able to program themselves to be human companions.*

## LIVING WITH BOTS

Hopefully, life will be peaceful and happy in the year 2250. Nanotechnology and self-assembling robots might have brought big changes to the environment, bringing water and crops to areas that, 200 years earlier, were struggling with drought and famine. In giant cities above and below ground, and in communities floating on the ocean or standing on the sea bed under it, robots might co-exist peacefully with people.

# ROBOTS RISING!

**R**elax. Robots today and in the near future pose no threat to us. They cannot think for themselves, or break out of their programming and safety overrides. Nor can they work together to rise up against people. Not yet, anyway!

## REBELLION!

The idea of robots turning on their masters goes back a long way. The first use of the term "robot" was in a 1920s' Czech play, *R.U.R. (Rossum's Universal Robots)* by Karel Capek. It painted a bleak picture of robots rebelling and enslaving humans.

*Robosaurus is a fire-breathing, car- and plane-crushing robot dinosaur built for entertainment. What if machines like this could think for themselves? Would they rebel against humans?*

## ROBOGEDDON!

Scientists today think it's unlikely that future robots would be able to organize an Earth-wide rebellion and take over the planet, but let's just imagine…

By 2350, robots with true artificial intelligence may be serving humans in the military. Battlefields may be entirely robotic, with humans far from the front line. What's to stop robots from deciding that they no longer want to risk danger in the service of their human masters? What if a robot army refuses to fight, or decides to join forces with the enemy?

In a future world, powerful robots and computers may be employed to run entire countries. What if they calculate that serving people is not the best way of running the planet? Earth might never be the same again.

*In the film Terminator, humans in 2029 fight a war against robots, such as the near-indestructible T-800s.*

## ARMED MACHINES

Ten years ago, the idea of arming robots seemed unthinkable, but today it is a reality. These days, some military robots have deadly weapons. The Talon mobile rover, for example, can be fitted with a machine gun, grenade launcher or anti-tank rocket. Weapon-wielding robots have also taken to the air. Unmanned Combat Aerial Vehicles (UCAVs), such as the Northrop Grumman X-47 and the Dassault nEUROn, are flying military robots. UCAVs are cheaper than normal jets and, since they have no pilots, can be sent on more dangerous missions. Future UCAVs might even hunt in packs!

*With its caterpillar tracks, the Talon can trundle over rough ground for miles.*

## ENSLAVED BY BOTS

A robot uprising could be brutal and brief, or long and drawn-out. Either way, robots with super powers of reasoning might decide that there are easier ways than combat to get control from humans.

By 2350, robots may be involved in so many aspects of human life that they could secure victory simply by sabotaging water, power, food or medical supplies. Would robots then enslave humans? It's unlikely, since people would not be able to match the efficiency and skills of these incredible thinking machines. The likely outcome is chilling: some humans of use might be kept, but what would become of those humans for whom no use can be found?

# THE THREE LAWS OF ROBOTICS

*In* Runaround, *a short story first published in 1942, science-fiction writer Isaac Asimov devised the three laws that all robots would be programmed to obey at all times. Other writers and films went on to explore what would happen if robots disobeyed these laws.*

**THE FIRST LAW:** A robot may not injure a human being or, through inaction, allow a human being to come to harm.

**THE SECOND LAW:** A robot must obey orders given to it by human beings except where such orders would conflict with the First Law.

**THE THIRD LAW:** A robot must protect its own existence as long as such protection does not conflict with the First or Second Law.

## DID YOU KNOW?

An American robotic gun platform called Trap-2 can track its target and fire a rifle with pinpoint accuracy – hitting a 2.5-cm (1-in) target each and every time from 100 m (328 ft) away.

*This brand-new Battlefield Extraction and Retrieval Robot (BEAR) is designed to find, lift and rescue wounded soldiers.*

# ROBOTS MOST WANTED

The human race will never be safe with these evil robot creations from movies on the loose!

### MARIA

**Source:** *Metropolis* (1927, movie)
**Location:** Earth, 2026

Maria, an evil robot replica of a good and honest woman, almost destroys the city of Metropolis by causing rebellion among its workers. She is caught and burned, when her metal body is revealed.

### GORT

**Source:** *The Day the Earth Stood Still* (1951, movie)
**Location:** Earth, 1950s

This huge, law-enforcing robot accompanies the alien Klaatu on a mission to stop human aggression. When the guns are turned on Klaatu, Gort shuts down the world's power supplies.

### MEGATRON

**Source:** *Transformers* (2007, movie), TV series and magazines
**Location:** Earth and the planet Cybertron, 2007

Leader of the Decepticons, Megatron is powerful, very aggressive and utterly ruthless. His main weapon is his arm-mounted fusion cannon, which is capable of destroying a whole city block in one blast. He can also fire electrical blasts from his hands and laser shots from his eyes.

### NS-5

**Source:** *I, Robot* (2004, movie)
**Location:** Earth, 2035

These ultimate home robots are programmed to abide by the three laws of robotics (*see above left*) until V.I.K.I., the computer that uploads software into each NS-5, forces them to turn on their human masters.

### TERMINATOR T-800

**Source:** *The Terminator* (1984, movie)
**Location:** Earth, 1984 and 2029

This robot is sent from the year 2029 to assassinate the mother of a future human leader. It is encased in a human-like skin, but runs on hydrogen power cells that last 120 years.

# GLOSSARY

**AGVs (Automated Guided Vehicles)**
Robotic vehicles without a driver that follow a set path in a factory, hospital or office.

**AI (Artificial intelligence)** Intelligence given to robots and computers to make them capable of thinking and learning.

**automata** Mechanical devices that imitate the movements of a person or living creature.

**autonomous machine** A machine that works by itself without human help.

**blimp** A small airship used chiefly for observing the ground below.

**byte** A measure of computer memory. There are 1,024 bytes in a kilobyte, and 1,024 kilobytes in 1 megabyte.

**circuit board** A board used to link electronic parts together.

**consumer products** Products, such as TVs and cars, that are bought by people.

**controller** The device on a robot that receives information from the robot's sensors and instructs other parts of the robot.

**cyborg** A creature that combines human parts and abilities with machine ones.

**degrees of freedom** The different directions in which a robot arm can move.

**end-effector** The tool at the end of a robot arm that performs tasks, such as gripping.

**exoskeleton** A skeleton on the outside of a creature or machine.

**flight recorder** A system in a box that records the details of an aircraft flight.

**gears** Parts of a machine – often interlinking wheels - that help to control speed.

**humanoid** A robot that looks or performs like a human.

**hydraulics** A system of pistons and cylinders that helps move things, such as robot parts.

**International Space Station (ISS)**
A large spacecraft orbiting the Earth that robots have helped to build.

**mass-produce** To build large numbers of a product, usually in a factory.

**microprocessor** A tiny computer inside a robot that acts as the controller.

**microchip** A collection of microscopic electrical circuits fitted to a single wafer of a substance called "silicon". Also called a "chip".

**microsurgery** Surgery performed inside the body using tiny tools and cameras.

**nanobots** Incredibly tiny robots that could be made in the future by nanotechnology.

**nanotechnology** The science of making machines measured in nanometres. A nanometre is a millionth of a millimetre.

**NASA (the National Aeronautics and Space Administration)** The organization that plans and runs America's space missions.

**nuclear power** A type of energy given out from nuclear fusion (the splitting of atoms).

**pneumatics** A system that uses air under pressure to move something, such as a robot.

**program** A series of instructions that control or operate a computer or a robot.

**programmable** Describes a machine that can accept and follow a series of instructions.

**radioactive** Giving out a type of energy that can harm living things.

**robot swarm** A collection of robots that all work together in some way to perform a task.

**ROVs (Remote-Operated Vehicles)**
Underwater robots controlled by an operator from a distance.

**sensor** A device inside a robot that collects information about the robot or its surroundings.

**service robots** Robots that work in non-industrial fields and help humans by acting as robotic gardeners, cleaners or receptionists.

**silicon chip** Another name for a microchip.

**silicone** A rubbery substance used to make a robot material that resembles human skin.

**solar panel** A collection of solar cells that convert sunlight into electrical energy.

**space probes** Scientific machines sent into space to travel past or land on planets, moons and other objects in space.

**terraform** To change the conditions and environment of a planet to make it suitable for humans to live on.

**thermal imager** A camera that detects heat rather than light. It can be used at night-time to produce a heat picture of a scene.

**touchscreen** A device where options are displayed on a flat screen and can be chosen by touching the screen.

**tranquillizer dart** A small, pointed arrow covered with a drug that causes sleep.

**transmit** To send a signal. In robotics, this is often an electrical or radio signal.

**transistor** An electrical component that switches an electric current on or off or makes it greater.

**UAVs (Unmanned Aerial Vehicles)**
Flying robots that are either remote-controlled or can fly by themselves.

**voltage** The force, measured in volts, of an electric currrent.